Schaum Fingerpower

POP
LEVEL FOUR

10 PIANO SOLOS
WITH TECHNIQUE WARM-UPS

Arranged by JAMES POTEAT

The purpose of the Fingerpower Pop series is to provide musical experiences beyond the traditional **Fingerpower®** books. The series offers students a variety of popular tunes, including hits from today's pop charts as well as from classic movie themes, beloved Broadway shows, and more! The arrangements progress in order of difficulty, and technique warm-ups are included for each solo.

CONTENTS

ISBN 978-1-5400-3481-6

EXCLUSIVELY DISTRIBUTED BY
HAL•LEONARD®

Visit Hal Leonard Online at
www.halleonard.com

Contact us:
Hal Leonard
7777 West Bluemound Road
Milwaukee, WI 53213
Email: info@halleonard.com

In Europe, contact:
Hal Leonard Europe Limited
42 Wigmore Street
Marylebone, London, W1U 2RN
Email: info@halleonardeurope.com

In Australia, contact:
Hal Leonard Australia Pty. Ltd.
4 Lentara Court
Cheltenham, Victoria, 3192 Australia
Email: info@halleonard.com.au

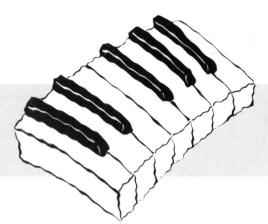

WARM-UPS

Warm-Up for
"Try Everything"
(page 14)

WRIST STACCATO with SYNCOPATION
Count carefully, and build to a faster pace.

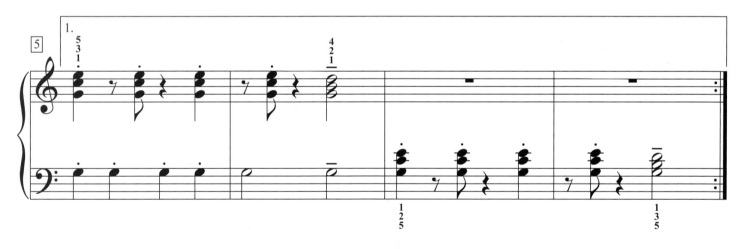

Warm-Up for
"A Thousand Years"
(page 17)

CROSS-HAND ARPEGGIOS
Use pedal.

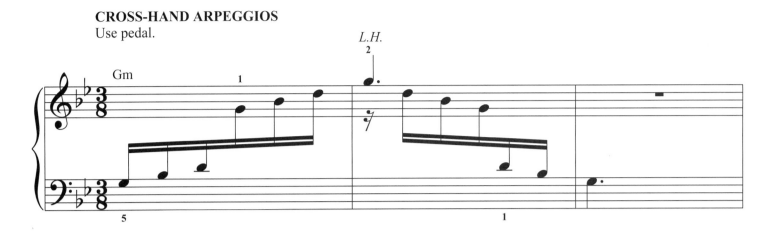

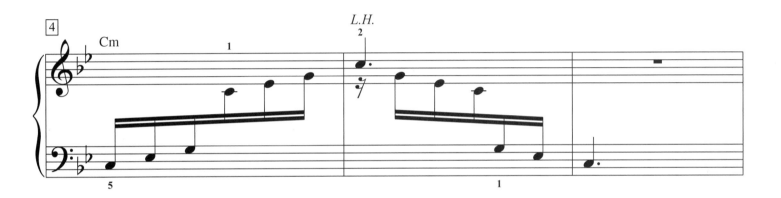

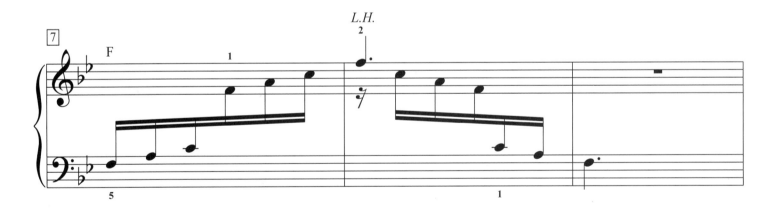

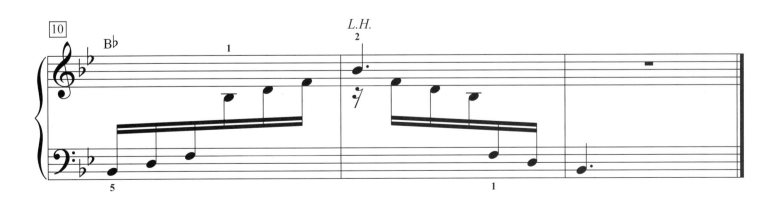

Warm-Ups for
"Stand by Me"
(page 20)

1. LEAPS for the LEFT HAND

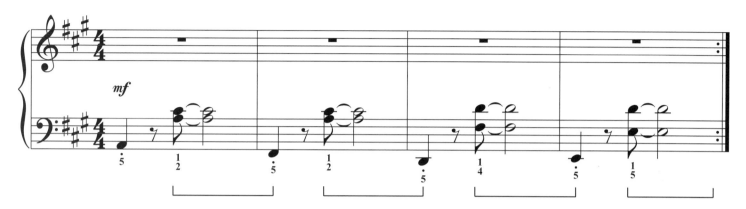

2. LARGER LEAPS for the LEFT HAND

3. RIGHT-HAND RHYTHM
Use the left hand's steady quarter notes as a helpful guide.

Warm-Ups for
"Piano Man"
(page 23)

1. BLUES SCALE

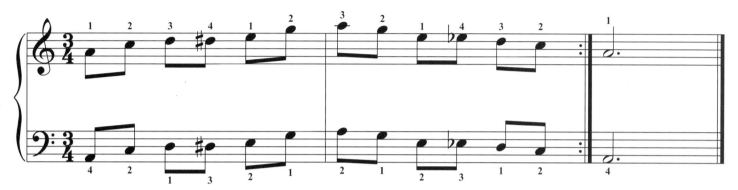

2. CHORD PROGRESSION DOWN the C SCALE
Use fingers 1, 3, and 5 except where marked.
Practice with and without pedal.

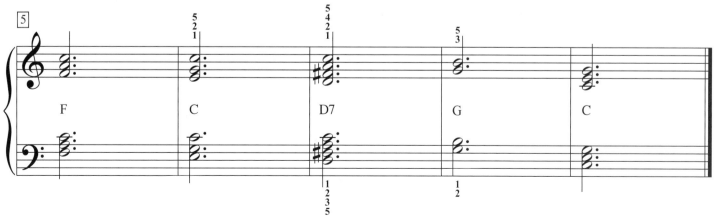

Warm-Ups for
"Radioactive"
(page 26)

1. RIGHT-HAND RHYTHM
Use the left hand's steady quarter notes as a helpful guide.

2. EXTENDED ARPEGGIOS
Play legato, and practice with and without pedal.

Warm-Up for
"Smile"
(page 28)

DOUBLE GRACE NOTES

Warm-Ups for
"Blackbird"
(page 30)

1. TURNS

2. CHROMATIC HAND CONTRACTION

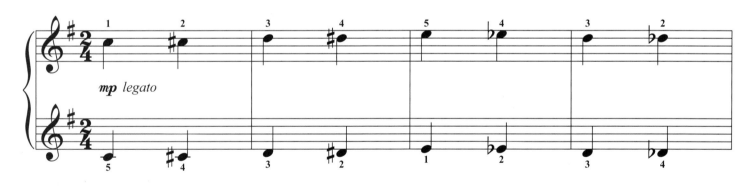

Warm-Ups for
"We Know the Way"
(page 32)

1. RIGHT-HAND RHYTHM
Use the left hand's steady quarter notes as a helpful guide.
Practice with and without pedal.

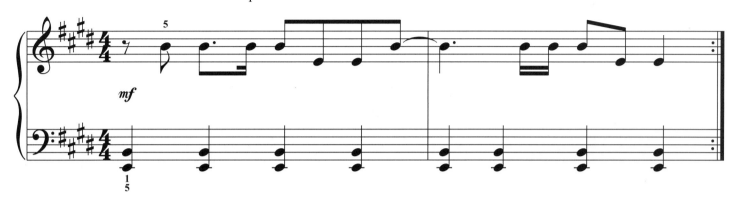

2. LEGATO
Keep the upper notes legato as you shift the R.H. thumb.
Play without pedal.

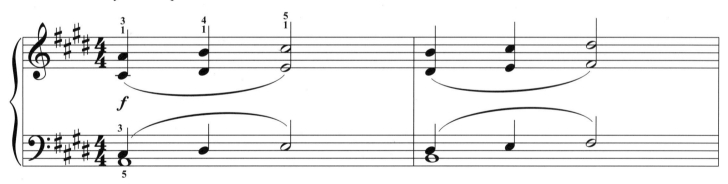

Warm-Up for
"I Feel the Earth Move"

(page 34)

RIGHT-HAND RHYTHM
Use the left hand's steady quarter notes as a guide.

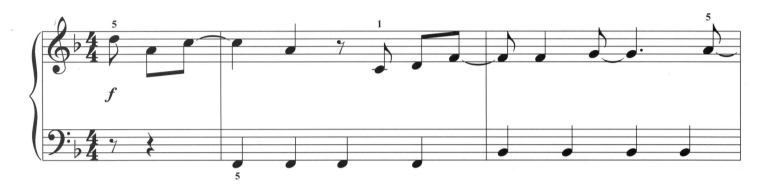

Warm-Ups for "Defying Gravity"
(page 36)

1. LEFT-HAND CHORD PROGRESSION
Pay special attention to the rhythm and the fingering.

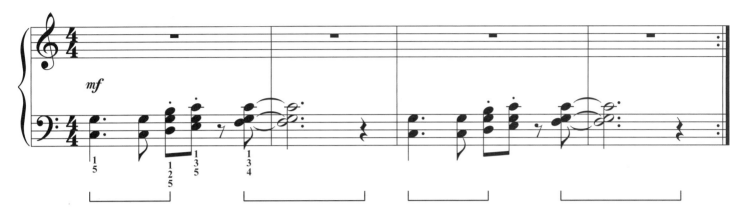

2. RIGHT-HAND RHYTHM
Use the left hand's steady quarter notes as a helpful guide.

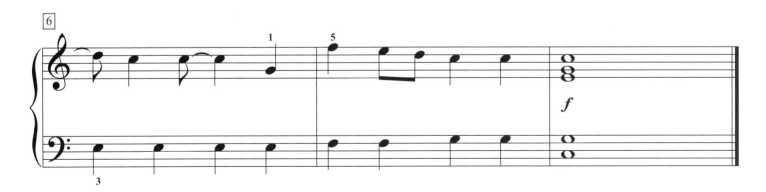

SOLOS

Try Everything
from ZOOTOPIA

Words and Music by Sia Furler,
Tor Erik Hermansen and Mikkel Eriksen
Arranged by James Poteat

WARM-UP: page 2

Pulsing ♩ = 112

A Thousand Years

from the Summit Entertainment film THE TWILIGHT SAGA: BREAKING DAWN - PART 1

Words and Music by David Hodges
and Christina Perri
Arranged by James Poteat

WARM-UP: page 3

Deliberately ♪ = 132

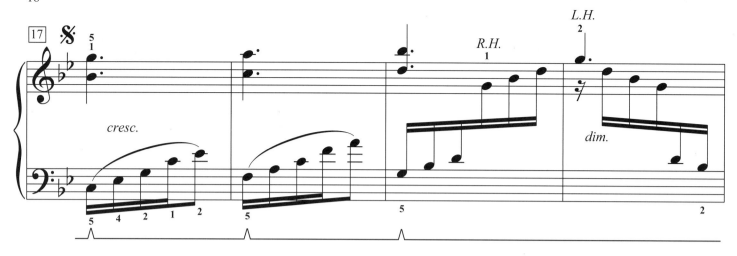

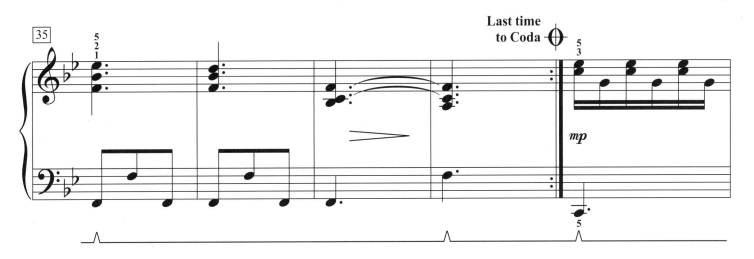

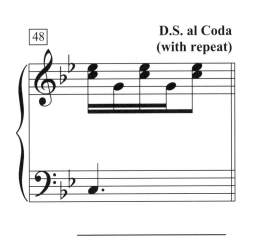

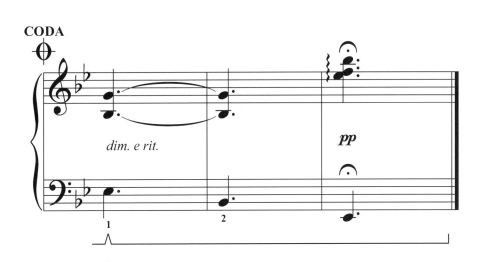

Stand by Me

WARM-UP: page 4

Words and Music by Jerry Leiber,
Mike Stoller and Ben E. King
Arranged by James Poteat

ped. simile

Piano Man

Words and Music by
Billy Joel
Arranged by James Poteat

WARM-UP: page 5

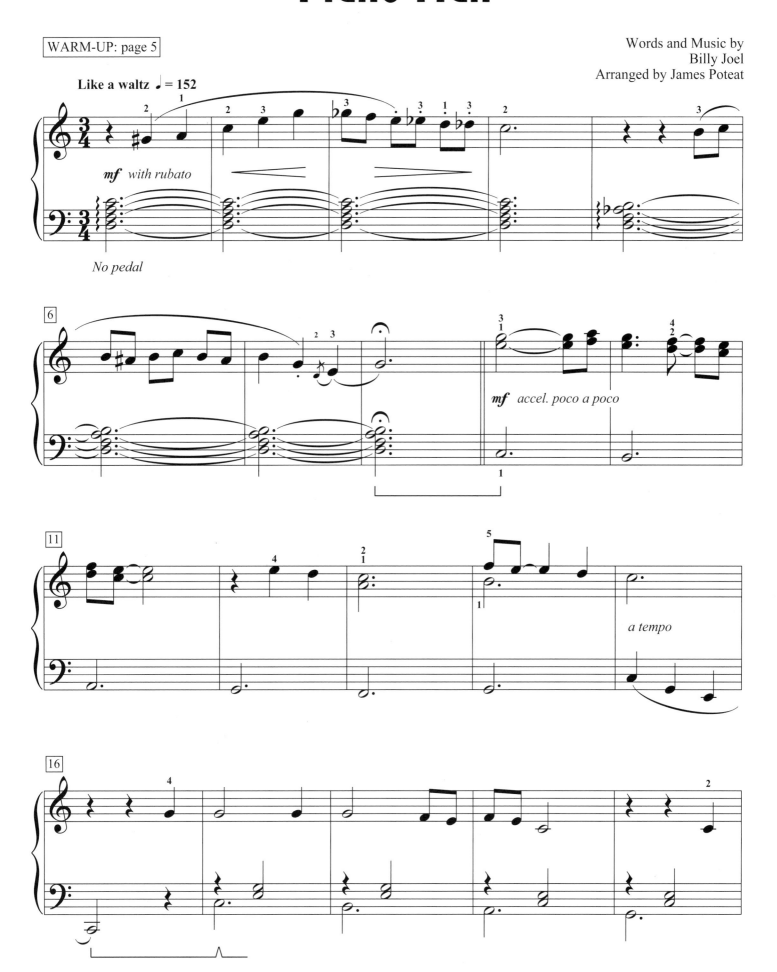

Radioactive

Words and Music by Daniel Reynolds,
Benjamin McKee, Daniel Sermon,
Alexander Grant and Josh Mosser
Arranged by James Poteat

WARM-UP: page 6

Smile
Theme from MODERN TIMES

WARM-UP: page 7

Words by John Turner and Geoffrey Parsons
Music by Charles Chaplin

Slowly ♩ = c. 54

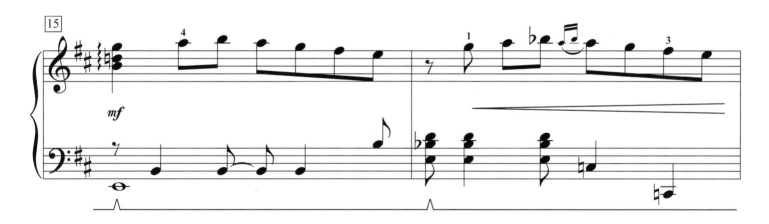

Blackbird

WARM-UP: page 8

Words and Music by John Lennon
and Paul McCartney
Arranged by James Poteat

We Know the Way
from MOANA

WARM-UP: page 9

Music by Opetaia Foaʻi
Lyrics by Opetaia Foaʻi and Lin-Manuel Miranda
Arranged by James Poteat

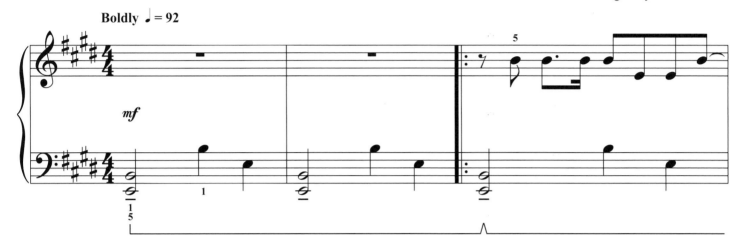

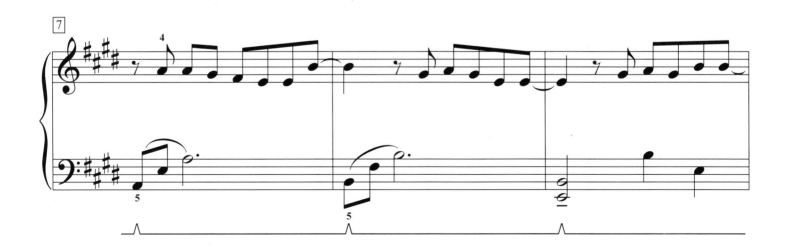

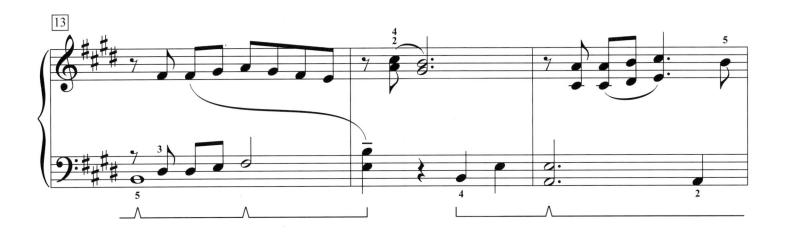

I Feel the Earth Move

WARM-UP: page 10

Words and Music by
Carole King
Arranged by James Poteat

Defying Gravity
from the Broadway Musical WICKED

Music and Lyrics by
Stephen Schwartz
Arranged by James Poteat

WARM-UP: page 11

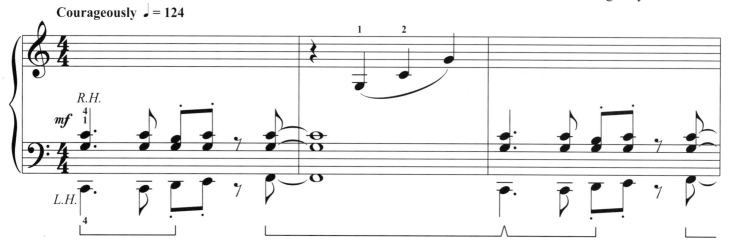

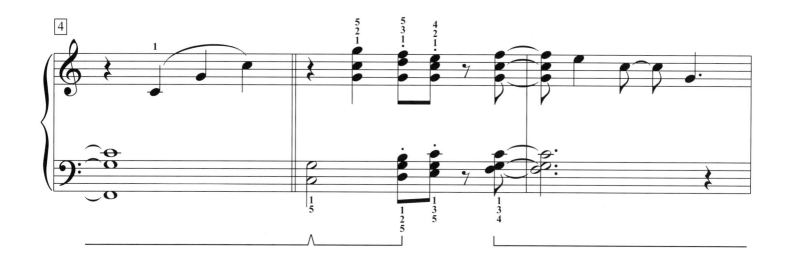

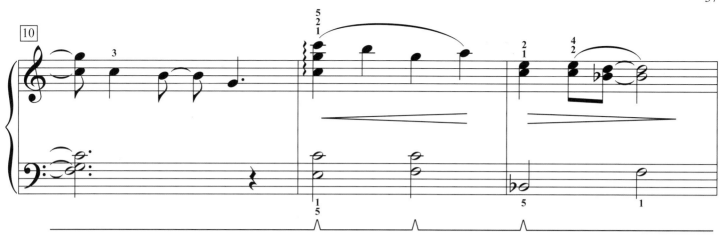

ABOUT THE ARRANGER

Since 2007 **James Poteat** has taught piano, trombone, euphonium, music theory, and composition in Woodstock, Georgia. Mr. Poteat works with students of all ages and skill levels and is equally comfortable in the worlds of popular and classical music. James is constantly arranging music for his students and is dedicated to creating and using materials of the highest quality. Learn more about James and his work by visiting **www.musicalintentions.com**.